THE FOOTBALL CORPORATIONS

Also by William Heyen

Poetry

Depth of Field (1970, 2005)
Noise in the Trees: Poems and a Memoir (1974)
The Swastika Poems (1977)
Long Island Light: Poems and a Memoir (1979)
The City Parables (1980)
Lord Dragonfly: Five Sequences (1981, 2010)
Erika: Poems of the Holocaust (1984)
The Chestnut Rain (1986)
Brockport, New York: Beginning with "And" (1988)
Pterodactyl Rose: Poems of Ecology (1991)
Ribbons: The Gulf War (1991)
The Host: Selected Poems 1965-1990 (1994)
Crazy Horse in Stillness (1996)
Diana, Charles, & the Queen (1998)
Shoah Train (2003)*
The Rope (2003)
The Confessions of Doc Williams & Other Poems (2006)*
To William Merwin: A Poem (2007)
A Poetics of Hiroshima (2008)*
The Angel Voices (2010)
Straight's Suite for Craig Cotter & Frank O'Hara (2012)
Hiroshima Suite (2012)

Prose

Vic Holyfield & the Class of 1957: A Romance (1986)
With Me Far Away: A Memoir (1994)
Pig Notes & Dumb Music: Prose on Poetry (1998)
The Hummingbird Corporation (2003)
Home: Autobiographies, Etc. (2004)
Titanic & Iceberg: Early Essays & Reviews (2005)
The Cabin: Journal 1964–1984 (2012)

Anthologies

A Profile of Theodore Roethke (Ed. 1971)
American Poets in 1976 (Ed. 1976)
The Generation of 2000: Contemporary American Poets (Ed. 1984)
September 11, 2001: American Writers Respond (Ed. 2002)*

*Asterisks indicate titles also published by Etruscan Press.

THE FOOTBALL CORPORATIONS

poems

WILLIAM HEYEN

etruscan press

Etruscan Press
Wilkes University
84 West South Street
Wilkes-Barre, PA 18766
(570) 408-4546

WILKES UNIVERSITY

www.etruscanpress.org

Published 2012 by Etruscan Press
Printed in the United States of America
Cover design by Robert Carioscia and Julianne Popovec
Interior design by Julianne Popovec
The text of this book is set in Palatino Linotype.
Cover art: Robin Selditch

First Edition

12 13 14 15 16 5 4 3 2 1

Library of Congress Cataloging-in-Publication Data

Heyen, William, 1940-
 The football corporations : poems / William Heyen.
     p. cm.
 ISBN 978-0-9832944-5-0 (alk. paper)
 1. Sports--Poetry. I. Title.
 PS3558.E85F66 2012
 811'.54--dc22

Please turn to the back of this book for a list of the sustaining funders
of Etruscan Press.

This book is printed on recycled, acid-free paper.

For Tyler Gregorio, Xerxes, Coach Ruskus, Statics, Steed, Gilderflash, Shabazz, Typhoon, Tank Galahad, Jamal, Rune, Jesus, Joe D., Wild Bill Hickok, Eddie Felsen, Seamus, Chantel, Druga, Josh Porko, Maria Ortiz, Snake Plissken, 44, Stryker, Arroyo, & all the others.

THE FOOTBALL CORPORATIONS

I. *Competition*

In Memoriam	7
Competition	8
Coma	9
Still Life	10
The Fumble	11
Stats	12
Chantel's Secret	13
Shabazz	15
After the Game	16
The Trophy	17
Autopsy	18
Online	19
Rain	20
Draft	21
The Cranberry Corporation	22
Curling	23
Election	24
Recording Transcript: The Hospital	25
Credentials	26

II. *Romance*

Romance	29
Shrines	30
Last Call	31
Home Stand	32
Union Church	33
If Jesus Played Football	34

Oh Joy   35
Homecoming   36
The Altercation   37
The Girl   38
Opening Day   39
Triple Play   40
The American Novel   41
Heaven   42
Arena Cuts: *Escape from New York*   43
Image   45
Rack   46
Little League Pastoral   47
The Smithtown Indians, 1953   48
Pop Quiz   49
Sloshed, Old Brooklyn, 1940   50
Rood   51
Publicity   52
Logo   53
Home Ice   54
Beautiful Maria   55
The Past   56
Epilogue   57
Allegiances   58

III. *The Football Corporations*

Anthem Flick   61
The Cloud   62
Spokesperson   63
Interim   64
The Reader   65
Age   66
For Now   68

Where We Were & What We Were Doing   69
Coliseum Souvenir   76
The Stadium   77
The Football Corporations   78
The Warrior   79
Capsule   80
Centennial   81
Yellow Card   82
Story   83

Acknowledgments

Grateful acknowledgments are made to the editors of the periodicals in which some of these poems previously appeared: *The Atlantic, Café Review, Chautauqua, Janus Head, The Kenyon Review, OnEarth, Poetrybay, Poetry Kanto* (Japan), *The Seventh Quarry* (Wales), *Together.*

"Stats" first appeared in the author's *The Confessions of Doc Williams & Other Poems* (Etruscan Press, 2006). "Chantel's Secret" first appeared in *Fast Break to Line Break: Poets on the Art of Basketball*, edited by Todd Davis (Michigan State University Press, 2011).

Preface

I don't know a scrum from a huddle, a power-play from a triple-play, a slider from a slice, a soccer ball from a football, a shot-blocker from a crackback block, but make no mistake: poetry has never been primarily a matter of what might be identified as its subject matter. I don't care much about World Cups or cups that protect jocks' nuts. But I'm fiercely interested in societal derangements of mania, force, greed. Beginning to end, *The Football Corporations*, often by way of the poet's various personae, places us at horse tracks & ice rinks, in locker rooms & gymnasia, in the geometries of courts & diamonds & pitches & gridirons, as Heyen, apparently a tough-guy ex-athlete himself, lets us in on what's going on beneath what seems to be going on as individuals form & feed corporations that provide spectacle that becomes, increasingly, in Karl Marx's woozy image, an "opiate" for the masses; yes, our religion dressed not in robes but in helmets & pads & sneaks & spikes, logos ablaze. But "Word is that maybe a few luckier dozens / fought their way through tunnels or locker rooms // out of that labyrinth beneath the stadium." As hooligans riot & nukes deploy, we'll huddle in the arena that is this book of revelations. We'll listen not to the loudspeaker of ostensible subject, but to the manager-poet's whispered prayers, & we might come out alive, armed with scores of insights to carry us beyond manipulation, beyond delusion.

—Edwina Seaver
Berlin / 2012

THE FOOTBALL CORPORATIONS

I. COMPETITION

IN MEMORIAM

The kid named Tyler cheated past the line,
& at the snap hurled himself into a blocker,
leveled him, then pulled down another,
then clawed at the ball carrier. No pads here,
no helmets, just blood & guts tackle
at the town park as evening touched down.

67, I stood behind chain-link, the only spectator,
but other kids congregated across the street.
All my life I've been an athlete, so believe me,
my fear here wasn't for concussions or fractured ribs,
but my childhood sun going down from when
I'd played football with mock-fierce friends
who were not out for one another's necks. "Break

his fucking spine," Tyler yelled before another snap,
& here's where I don't even want to think about
what happened next…. I remember my older brother
way back then got his nose busted, & remember
a brawl after some bullshit piling on, but then
handshakes & arm-wrestling later at the pizza joint.
But now, I had to turn my back & jog home,

a thousand yards away, my headset skull
filling with cuts of my beloved doo-wop.
The morning paper reports that the cops
broke up a drug bash at dawn & found
a dead teen, Tyler Gregorio, in a hammock.
A blood trail led them to the park.
My bookend trophies press against the dark.

COMPETITION

What happened was that Xerxes,
drunk &/or drugged after the upset,
side-swiped a parked police cruiser
with his customized Hummer, veered

over the curb, took out a fire hydrant,
a woman & her poodle, a fruit stand,
&, lastly, a couple of schoolkids
who fumbled their backpacks

about thirty yards, their papers aflutter
with watercolored families under
spoked sunshine, & animals in meadows
with huge smiles on their faces—

pigs, chickens, ducks, horses.
When cops pried open the Hummer's door,
the linebacker growled, "No autographs,"
then puked his own colors & fell into a coma.

Coda

When, after a decade, the linebacker woke,
lawyers argued whether or not he'd served his sentence—
justice vacillates from the unconscious to the conscious.
The league helps its property to inscribe his X.

COMA

Coach Ruskus had his mind elsewhere,
trying to lead his team in prayer,
when struck by his own pistol
in the chaos down there.

The hospital says he's in a coma,
that he'll be under for a while.
Subdural hematoma,
a clot between brain & skull.

They hope before long to operate,
but he might be a vegetable.
One minute, prayers; the next,
you're on the table.

A few have decided not to attend
one or more games this season,
but there's a waiting list for tickets,
& it's up to the corporations

as to when such violence
might end. The Board of Directors
isn't in any hurry. A press conference
is scheduled to announce

Ruskus' replacement. Rumor has it
that it's What's-his-name from Stalingrad
who pole-axed two fans a few years ago.
Ruskus will be the last to know.

STILL LIFE

A trainer found him in the locker room
   early morning before the game.

Statics was naked except for jock & socks,
   & the belt around his neck.

At first the trainer thought he was breathing—
   just shadows or something.

The coroner said he'd been dead for hours,
   maybe since last year

after he missed that kick. We still see that ball
   held up against the shearwall.

THE FUMBLE

At first the fumble seemed rigged, like Steed
coughed it up on purpose, but replays proved
Jackson's helmet speared the ball
on a perfect freak hit, and that was that. Still,

a million dumbnuts who never played the game
swear that Steed *coulda shoulda woulda* held on
despite that jolt from behind from Jackson
in his own backfield, on his own team.

Go talk to them if you don't believe me—
they spill their guts to anyone who asks.
I've never seen college athletes cry like this,
though Corporation pros have them beat.

STATS

When the All-American halfback broke through,
the middle linebacker struck off his head,
but Gilderflash hung onto the pigskin,
& kept running, his neck gushing blood

from between shoulder pads.
Except for a shotgun blast from the stands,
he'd have broken the goal-line plane, a record
for the most TDs by a dead Heisman.

CHANTEL'S SECRET

Chantel, 6-11 franchise center, wheeled & slammed, then
elbowed her defender in the neck, but
didn't get ejected.

The Axis coach exploded, but the refs showed discretion,
didn't axe him—maybe they knew
they'd been too lax,

maybe intimidated by Chantel who spent
most of the second half taunting
the enemy bench

every time she backpedaled after scoring, which was often,
until a last dunk when
a sub goon

undercut her. She went down like an imploding casino,
& caught fire, & from her bra,
ex-

tracted a box-cutter & went berserk—
she didn't kill anyone,
but cut tendons

& ligaments of two Axis benchwarmers
beyond repair, despite even
the wonders

of modern sports bionics. She might miss half a season
during which ratings will decline,
but this time

the league's got to suck it up at least to *seem*
to be doing something.
Chantel

has not yet expressed regret—she's as stoic
an athlete as they come—
but this time

she'd best keep close to her entourage & bodyguards
or the family of the maimed &/
or Axis fans

will take her out. All in all, it's a shame, isn't it,
that this fracas happened just before
the play-offs?—

now the record will require countless asterisks.
We'd like to be mice under the table
at Corporation headquarters

when Chantel's endorsement contracts are renegotiated.
Little will change, though that negligee
might be a hard-on sell.

SHABAZZ

St. John of the Cross, his "Cloud of Unknowing," sings chords
of mystical godhead,
thus Shabazz was listening to the audio before that last match
against Belgrade.

The words, half understood—Slavic was not his native language—
soothed him.
Yes, we are consoled that St. John comforted Shabazz before
his final competition.

What else was in his zPod, we've no way
of knowing unless
lawyers release this information, & this is far
from likely unless

there's strong torque from the Oval Office which is
loath to interfere
despite rumors that the President was there that day Shabazz
stood under the goalposts

like a god, no, like a humble disciple prepared to receive fate's
verdict of victory
or death. Now, praising him, some of us do not picture
his fractures or stigmata

that circled the world in those next hours, but Shabazz hunched over
in front of his locker,
listening to divine presence, arming himself for the only
struggle that mattered.

AFTER THE GAME

That famous photo of Typhoon with his head
between his knees with the flashback sun
from the mirror behind him just before
he fell forward & lay dead, just before

Corporation publicists ordered in more media
to spin their mantra that Typhoon, for his team,
continued to play hard despite concussions
in the first & second quarters, & in overtime.

What a shame he couldn't live to autograph
10,000 photos right across that sun
to swell the Corporation's bottom line
for his replacement, maybe that beast from Zion.

THE TROPHY

Befitting his nickname, Jockstrap collected cups,
sometimes sweat-stained from games,
sometimes flecked or splotched with blood,
which made him happy. But fame

only found him when he won that auction
for Tank Galahad's pellet-riddled styrofoam
from that Globe Bowl goal-line stand
when a stoned fan shot Tank to stop him.

That icon draws visitors to Jockstrap's museum
by the hundreds of thousands every season.
Too bad Tank didn't get to sign it,
but you can't get autographs from the dead,

though Tank's DNA did jack that cup up
like the Crown Jewels (all puns intended).

AUTOPSY

That last time Jamal rose to the basket, his head did
nick the rim, but it was a bullet
that did him in,

though at first no one knew it: the slug
penetrated his left armpit
& stayed hidden.

Webster, who was guarding him, later said that
he himself was in a zone, didn't
even hear the fans,

never mind a gunshot, which came, in any case,
through a silencer & from a distance.

Jamal's missed dunk rebounded back out beyond
the three-point line—

one quick pass & the game was over. Go figure
whether the refs should have called time
right when Jamal hit the floor,

or if that last lay-up was legit. Not that Webster fouled him,
but when a leaper lands on his back
& dies spasming like that,

stop the game ferchrissakes before bets go down the drain
like mine did. I hate even
thinking about it.

ONLINE

Rune hits the nuts on the river. Again
our main character, X-Man, clicks in
to call, this time with two pair which should,
of course, have won, except
that three others, too, were priced in,
& if Rune didn't river X-Man, then
it would have been another. In other words,
our hero was drawing to hit dead,
but didn't know it, & nothing will resurrect him,
ever, is our guess, he or the other addicts
who don't study but trust to intuition.
Tonight, X-Man is maxed out, & his woman
keeps nagging. Tomorrow, a tournament,
60,000 entrants, which he plans to win.

RAIN

The jock was holding back Go-For-Broke
in the sixth or I'm a horse's ass, man.
Whatever collusion the track's got going on,
you & I ain't part of it, & I'm sick
of betting dead money, I told you, man,
either we get in with these bastards,
or we don't, & if we don't we might as well
throw our dough into a urinal & piss on it.
We've got to get some kind of fucking access
when horses are worked out, or when jocks
bullshit their brains after their weigh-ins.
You know that florist, don't you, man,
who smells up this place before the races?
What's the chance you schmooze with him,
hang around stalls, listen to chatter,
keep your eyes open for injections,
get a read on what the fuck is going down?
No more of this confetti we keep scattering
into the weather. I'm fed up being busted
because these owners are paying jocks
to get themselves boxed in or break stride
or whip for show with one hand half as hard
as they pull back with the other.
Who you got in the eighth, man? Dreamer
looks good. He's supposed to be a mudder.

DRAFT

He's got what we call the right work ethic.
You know the gym rat cliché, first at practice,
last to leave. He says he wants to give back
to the game & to the Corporation,

so what's not to love about the kid. Forget
those college rape charges. He's got dough,
now, to keep fifty lawyers on retainer,
with plenty left to pay off half the city's

whores & groupies. Don't sweat
the small stuff. He's not even here yet
& we've sold out the season. Wait
till we talk TV. Let me propose a toast.

THE CRANBERRY CORPORATION

Tombé kneed Glickman in the nuts.
By the time the cops cleared the court,
both backboards had been ripped down,
& LoPresti's leg was broken.

This was the low point of a losing season,
but here's the important skinny:
Tombé said he was only sorry
he didn't kill the Jew, & Glickman yelled

that the nigger was a fag coward.
We've arranged their next meeting to be
Thanksgiving. TV is the League's gravy.
Thanks, boys, & please pass the turkey.

CURLING

So one dork slides a stone toward a bull's-eye
about a hundred feet down the ice & two dorks
skate like crazy with brooms & try to steer
the stone by sweeping in front of or to the side of it
or for all I know try to speed it or slow it
& ferchrissakes now this is an Olympic sport,
Milt, tell me what's next, maybe frisbee
or hula hoops or catching cats dropped from blimps,
which is something, in fact, I'd like to see
so as to hear them splat. I hope it's concrete,
& I'd sure boo the broad who wins the gold.

ELECTION

Rez tells me he don't see no difference between
the asterisked steroid sluggers &, say,
Mickey Mantle & Willie Mays, except vitamins.

But Rez, I says, steroids ain't vitamins,
there's no comparison. But such distinctions
ain't in Rez's strike zone, though every year he runs

for the school board. I count it pretty optimistic
that the town knows better than to vote him in.
The Mick & Willie. But that was then.

RECORDING TRANSCRIPT: THE HOSPITAL

Sir, I'm a security guard, I don't even
look at the game, I sit behind home bench
& face the other way, my eyes open

in case some dopehead or martyr
comes charging toward the ballplayers,
who are Corporation property. So I didn't see

what happened behind me, just heard a roar
& turned around in time to get a faceful
of blood. Everything came from the other

side of the court. I'll be glad, of course.
to cooperate. Right now, I need tests
& injections. You haven't allowed me

to phone my wife who watches TV
so now knows more than I do. I'm worried
about the blood, a possible infection….

Thanks for the sedative. I understand
that I won't be going anywhere until
both of us are positive I'm clean.

CREDENTIALS

For post-game interviews Mulvaney's perfect
with his arms crossed and his habit
of waiting maybe a full five seconds so that
he won't blurt anything to regret,

like What's-his-name a few seasons back
about quick-twitch-challenged Caucasians
who shouldn't oughta have a job except
Joe Beernuts expects to see himself on occasion.

Yeah, Mulvaney's safest for the Corporation,
I say let's give him what he wants
including the five-year extension
& that furniture, you know what I mean,

before he options for better weather
or that new franchise on the moon
with perks like a golf course in a crater
& bionics for his worn-out dong.

Who cares if he can't coach worth a damn? —
let his assistants take care of that.
We need his outer calm on teletron
after a lost War Bowl before our city's hit.

II. ROMANCE

ROMANCE

I was there, the gym quiet except for the sobs
of the girl writhing on the floor, & the sobs
of her mother who plunged from the bleachers
to kneel next to her to try to comfort her
while we all waited for the stretcher.

I see her on crutches, smiling, determined.
In one photo in my album, the quarterback,
her boyfriend, inscribes her cast.
I follow his stardom these days
during his scholarship while he performs

for State U. I sit close to her at games,
she flexes her knee a hundred times.
They're not together any more. In my dream,
I carry her books into the library,
& she is pregnant with our baby, or maybe

it's twins, we're not yet sure. Maybe
that's her mother sobbing in the aisle
from so much familial bliss.
My bride is sobbing in her wedding dress.
My best man passes me a perfect spiral.

SHRINES

Perfect timing: her hair skimming ice
in the beautiful death spiral, when the fan
shot her, his bullet entering her temple
at the aria's climactic moment, *"Vincerà,*
vincerà." Her partner first thought her skate
had lost its edge, & she'd gone limp
in despair. He held her dead weight,
expecting her to gather herself & rise,
but then saw blood, slashed to a stop,
& knelt to her as her murderer
was surrounded, beaten, taken to jail.
He confesses nothing that enlightens or consoles.
The usual apartment of photos & votive candles.
Every week, someone remembers her grave with roses.

LAST CALL

Look, okay, when OJ offed that broad
we didn't want to know what happened—
he was in a blood frenzy,
stabbing her & almost cutting off her head.
That guy Goldman just got in the way.
It's too maniacal to think about,

so we were glad the shrunken glove didn't fit
so he'd beat the rap so we could blame some
retard or psycho, some schizoid doper
for doing what was done, not Simpson, not
32 with his movie star smile & 2000 yards
in one season. Go visit the Buffalo Bills' stadium

before they raze it, check out the hero's name
in letters six feet high against the upper tier
& let it go at that. & what about that cop
who got disgraced in court? He ended up
in big money with his book about that Kennedy
who killed a girl with a baseball bat or maybe

golf club years before. More lives bogeyed,
& the Juice tees off with his bad knees.
You think there's justice? Don't ask her kids.
You ever see how beautiful she was, the blonde?
She lost the coin flip when they got hitched.
Forget it. One more brew & let's hit the road.

HOME STAND

During the seventh inning stretch, right after
"if they don't win it's a shame," a fan
fell on his own from, or was thrown from,
the upper tier

in center field. He didn't kill anyone, thank god,
but did fracture Mr. Balloon Man's arm
& loosed a couple dozen animals & hearts
to the roof of our dome

where they enjoyed their freedom & symbolism
for two or three games before losing helium
& descending, some said like heavenly bodies,
some, like souls.

UNION CHURCH

Just after their coach sat down to eat with them,
I counted twelve jocks at their training table.
Twilight washed in through a stained-glass transom.
They leaned toward him as he began to mumble.

IF JESUS PLAYED FOOTBALL

he'd be an end.
He'd lope out under the long,
impossible passes,
cradle them in his palms.
If he had to, he'd dive for them,
his fingers claiming that space
between ball & ground.
On short routes, his feints
& precise cuts
would fake the defense
out of their cleats;
on his feet, still running,
in a moment of communion,
he'd knock off their helmets
with a stiff arm.

Once in for six,
he'd spike the old pigskin.
In that spot would sprout a rose,
or a sunflower.
By the time time ran out,
both end zones would bloom
with roses & sunflowers.
After his shower,
he'd appear beside us
to pose for pictures.
He'd invite us home, we'd glide
from the stadium together
until the next game—
happy, undefeated, unafraid—
if Jesus played football.

OH JOY

Before the most memorable game of his life, the slugger's mother—
she had to insist her way into the clubhouse—brought him a gift
of *suzumuchi*, crickets, which she knew would have been hard for
him to find in Tokyo. Sadaharu Oh bowed, & when she left, held
her package to his ear. Yes, they were alive. He felt & heard their
wing-whirr….

Turmoil—vibrations of thousands shaking the stadium,
waving banners, chanting his name—began to dissolve … into
the sound of the insects, &, as he says in *A Zen Way of Baseball*, into
"the immense silence that their voices invoked."…

Before his first major league game, a coach had told him to
see the pitch with the eye in his hip. Imagine, as Sadaharu swings
this day, crickets singing that eye open to the way!

HOMECOMING

The best part of the game was when at halftime
the Assistant Athletic Director told the Athletic Director
they were through, & the latter smacked the former
right in the kisser. Then some grad assistants of theirs,
there to assist with the award ceremonies
meant to recognize several alumni All-Americans,
got into it, & easels & tables of plaques & medals
got knocked over, & in the general melee the dyke
at the mic kept crying *ladies please women women*
but no one listened & Dean Hapgood & the ADD & the AD
couldn't hardly get torn apart even by the All-Americans
but demonstrated various wrestling maneuvers legal
& illegal like hair pulling, choke holds, triple nelsons,
until Campus Security arrived full force to restore order
& all three were led off cuffed to our standing ovation.

THE ALTERCATION

What in hell's up with these young coaches?—
pass by their offices, they're at computers,
jawing to their players about stuff
no one ever learned except on the field

or court or in the pool or on the mat.
Choreographed mumbo-jumbo crap & make-believe.
Today, assistant line coach Bullock calls me
to take a look at some offensive tackle moves

on-screen. Arrows appear, & "trajectories,"
as Bullock calls them, "directionals," "virtual schematics."
"Jesus H. Lombardi give me a kid who wants to break
another kid's ribs with a crackback block

& you can keep this pansy-ass software, Bullock,"
I says. Then he winks & asks me if when I played
did we use helmets, & how many points for a dropkick?
I smacked him upside the head before Bronk broke us up.

THE GIRL

Don't tell me Hatfield weren't trying to break
McCoy's leg when he busted up the double play.
He weren't going in spikes normal, but spikes down,
& hard, & had the angle. We could hear
the crack from behind the backstop. McCoy's sister
screamed, Hatfield's old man & three brothers

got up pronto & headed for their pickups where
Goober says they keep a whole goldanged arsenal.
The teams fought, young McCoy owes the sawbones,
them Hatfields berl in their holler waiting for whatever.
You know the craziest one is that McCoy uncle.
He & that Hatfield girl hain't been seen all summer.

OPENING DAY

The President phones with congrats.
The famous coach isn't gaga this time
but pissed at being interrupted
from spraying bubbly with his team,

but thinking, too, This is the man, what the hell,
the man, … so when an invite is ordered
to visit the White House, he says they'd be glad
to check out the Prez's passing & punting skills….

Look ahead to see them on the lawn:
the war prexie dons a jersey, takes a hand-
off from the quarterback & strikes that straight-
arm running back's pose. The pros go home

with lucite paperweights bearing the great seal
of these United States, & photos for their dens.
American homes average three televisions.
This is your remote. Click to baseball.

TRIPLE PLAY

President Slickman at a reception
with only ten businessmen, & myself,
& my future ex, a senator's Head of Staff.
He tells us that just that afternoon
he'd lunched with hammering Hank Aaron.
He says he asked 44's opinion:
"Who was the greatest who ever played?"

Now the Prez enfolds his rapt listeners—
"Let me pose to y'all this question:
Who do you think Hank named?"
"Babe Ruth," barks one CEO. "DiMaggio,"
another. Slickman keeps shaking his mane.
"Willie Mays," my wife offers.
Slick nods & brushes up against her.

THE AMERICAN NOVEL

The starting point guard sits in front of me in class.
One morning after another close loss,
she roused from her trance

to interrupt the prof to say that William Faulkner,
unlike Hemingway, seems wild,
out of control, for better

or worse, almost loses possession—is this the genius
of his imagination. From there we began
driving the lane.

HEAVEN

Henry Thoreau's last words: "Moose ... Indian."
Joe DiMaggio's: "I'll finally get to see Marilyn."

Henry died never having gone to bed with a woman.
Joe enjoyed dozens, but in the end loved only one,

& believed that after he'd signed his last ball or bat,
he'd find her waiting in Yankee Stadium in starlight.

Henry died younger, & wasn't sure about the out-there,
except it sounded transcendentally beautiful, whether

or not it was cognizant of him or was just a cowbell
thunking in the mind of the great Oversoul,

but if it at least proved amenable
to hounds, bay horses, turtle doves, what the hell.

Maybe Henry's in Joe's penthouse, Joe in Henry's cabin,
maybe Joe is writing books, Henry hugging Marilyn,

maybe Henry is hitting homers, & Joe is fishing Walden,
maybe Joe & Hank are pals, & Marilyn ecstatic with Emerson.

ARENA CUTS: *ESCAPE FROM NEW YORK*

Plissken's first words: "Call me Snake."
Like he gives a fuck....

Three taps, three taps, then four
on manhole covers,

then three—metrical signals to the Crazies
that it's night, & to rise.

Soon it's Cabbie drives Snake from the grave
with his Molotov.

Brain's faithful melancholy babe Maggie with her
futuristic breasts

but no kids but us anywhere near here
to milk her....

The Duke cruising our *noir* city, chandeliers
mounted on his fenders—

"You meet him once," Cabbie says,
and then you're dead."...

Our brave hostage President whose ass
Plissken preserves

in the interest not of patriotics
but his own ticking neck....

Brain's home, NYPL, Alex-
andria, X....

Snake descends from the ring, the vanquished giant
behind him slumped

on the ropes with a gladiator's spiked club
nailed to his head....

Our night, black romance, patch over our hero's
blue iris.

I, Ishmael, neglected on purpose to mention:
all Manhattan—

as Snake exits with disdain—
is our prison.

IMAGE

At poker last night Dan Ricci, who is usually quiet,
took a pot with aces & eights, then said
everybody's heard

that Wild Bill was holding them when he got shot but
sources differ on whether or not
all four cards were black;

also, that when Jack McCall's bullet exited Bill's head it made
the sign of the cross on his temple,
& all those who saw it

figured it portended something dire, especially a preacher
who'd been raving at the bar. Dan said
Hickok seemed branded,

the cross seemed seared into him when the blood dried.
Here it burns, now, bluffing from where
Wild Bill is buried.

RACK

I knew Walter Tevis, who wrote *The Hustler*
while in grad school at the University of Iowa.

In the novel, Fast Eddie gets his hands broken—
the same as in the movie, where he's Paul Newman,

who spent a year at Ohio U., my own alma mater,
before dropping out for his Hollywood career.

I heard that in Iowa City, Walt's contract shone
on display in a bookstore shrine.

Christ, that fat Jackie Gleason could act,
even just chalking up his cue. In fact,

in sentimental TV skits, when Jackie played Poor Soul,
my old man misted up, who was no fool.

What about Paul, pal, & you, & me?
We all scratch, except Poor Soul & Eddie.

LITTLE LEAGUE PASTORAL

That day of the Nassau-Suffolk All-Star game
I dove from rocks & strained my groin.
I pitched that evening, but couldn't lift
my leg for speed. Nassau hit me pretty good—

no big deal in 1951. I don't think
my parents were even there,
& the ump worked in dungarees.
At bat, I doubled—the ball bounced

over a barbed-wire fence in left-center.
I limped to second, & maybe, could be,
scored, but can't remember. Later,
we goofed off even though we lost,

& no one pitied us. Coach Louis Vion,
at seventy I dream of little league heaven.
You stand at the plate to welcome our team.
We're coming, Coach, we yell, & hook-slide home.

THE SMITHTOWN INDIANS, 1953

That scrimmage, Coach Oderkirk subbed himself in
to guard me, man to man:

on his first possession, he snapped the ball, hard,
into my face. I went down.

"Surround that ball," he ordered. My nose & split cheekbone
spurted blood.

Skinny, shy, a thirteen-year-old freshman, I began to cry.
From this next century,

I seem to remember teammates kneeling in sympathy around me,
but I'm not certain.

This far later I can hear other coaches call him "Dutch."
Oder = other, *Kirk* = church.

I wish I had that whole season on film, maybe to understand
what got into the bastard.

The answer exists forever in earthlight fastbreaking
with shadows. Amen.

POP QUIZ

Back in high school, big Pete Callahan,
my older sister's ex,
was screwing around in the locker room
when he fractured his coccyx,

broke his ass. Coach Mularz nearly
had a conniption fit,
seeing as how Pete was to be his starting center
that night against Northport,

& what was Pete doing in the shower
during English class?
Well, the stories went around about poker
& about Bess

who wept rivers in her bedroom & who
never did recover
from the cruel inspired jokes about a lover
who couldn't make doo-doo.

Those were the years. I stood high school maybe
half the time,
& what about you, & what about me
in that locker room?

SLOSHED, OLD BROOKLYN, 1940

My old man anchored the Krauts,
a Bethlehem Steel bowling team.
He remembered he averaged about 200—
better than good

in those days of warped wood
& pin-setters who nursed hangovers
&/or imbibed between frames as did
Little Petey the night a perfect game

was almost in the books, Pop
hooking for the pocket
for a twelfth strike when Petey,
before the ball hit, fell forward

& took out half the pins.
Pop's team was well lit,
as were their opponents,
a bunch of micks—

a fight verged about some bets,
but then Petey lifted his head
long enough to shout,
"Youse guys is all a bunch of dopes,"

which cracked them up, including Pop.
The krauts & micks closed that bar
like best friends, hands on shoulders,
singing German-Irish in their beer.

ROOD

At least the hooligans' fire in the stands
melted snow that diluted the blood
seeping from Seamus' scalp where he lay
like a goalie brained while trying to block
a penalty kick that kissed the net
that shook when his head struck the post.
At least the hooligans' fire melted snow
which diluted beer that mixed with gore
that seeped into concrete & wood on that day
the living remember scar by scar, & the dead
in their clubhouse who were trampled & burned
now sing like the sacking of Troy that redeemed
their sacred honor, & likewise their team's.

PUBLICITY

I'm telling you it warms the heart the way our local
fast-food places came together & opened their doors
to serve as makeshift morgues to receive bodies
from the city, & it inspired us to see long lines
of ambulances & police vehicles pull in & out
of Burger King & Wendy's & Taco Bell & Hardee's
& Bruegger's Bagels & Pizza Hut & White Castle
& KFC & Ponderosa & Chinese Pavilion, where
tables & booths served adequately
& staff fed emergency workers for free,

but I don't blame the papers & TV for seizing on
the moment nurse Eliza Perkins at one McDonald's un-
zipped a bodybag & was shocked to find
her grandfather Sam who'd been at the stadium without
Eliza's knowledge when the incident occurred.
It was the worst moment of her life, she said,
but also, somehow, the best, since, if it had to be,
then she was blessed that she was there to claim him.
For its part, McDonald's was extremely sad for Eliza,
a spokesperson said, & planned to name a salad after Sam.

LOGO

The great striker Druga carried a gold doubloon
in a secret pocket
sewn behind the corporate skull & crossbones

on his jersey. His autobiography explains that he realized
he was acting half crazy,
but if kidnapped planned to deflect his captors with this coin,

to tell them, before they beheaded him,
that he had more,
a hundred thousand more of these where this one came from....

Maybe this gold would save him. In any case, this comfort
is what he touched when we thought,
those three World Cups, he was pointing to his heart.

HOME ICE

I'm no goon, but when the rook high-sticked me
I skated away & then, when he got behind me,
turned & hit him with my forearm cast.
He dropped like he'd fallen from a luxury box.
I got busted up by their enforcer. That's hockey.

These play-offs, then maybe one more season,
then I'm outta here while I can still ambulate,
me with my steel shoulder & six remaining teeth.
I've saved my loonies since my first signing.
Mary & me, we've been thinking about moving

to somewhere where flowers bloom
most of the year, maybe Hawaii where
no one knows power plays from iguanas.
I'll bury my trophies under a backyard palm.
If reporters come for me, I'll play dumb.

Did I mean to kill that kid. Who in hell knows?—
I hit him hard as I've ever hit anything,
except roids & scotch for a couple years. I sent
regrets to his family, but I'd take him out again,
except the loss cost me & the Corporation plenty,

including home ice. I dreamed last night
that my own goalie morphed
into a monster who resembled Frankenstein,
electrodes crackling in his cranium.
The last thing I did was turn my back on him.

BEAUTIFUL MARIA

Josh Porko hit home runs in his first two at-bats
in the World Baseball Classic, then got helmeted.
Dugouts emptied, a few players got upended,
but it was all just a wrestling match until
Miguel Ortiz stomped his spikes down hard
on Porko's temple. A cop phalanx got Porko's body
off the field pronto, but fans rioted in the stands

(even before learning that the great JP was dead),
then torched the stadium. The Corporation
considered canceling the Classic for a few years,
or perhaps two, or at least one, but then settled
on required seminars for umpires who must learn,
a spokesman said, "to anticipate, and defuse,
problematic situations." There on the teletron

coalesced Porko's grieving widow, red rose in ebon hair,
drawing her shawl tight, praying in English,
then Spanish, then tongues, for forgiveness for Miguel.
Josh's spirit, she said, demanded strength from her,
& for the Classic to continue. We knew she'd been
properly compensated, but in our memory Maria
is a saint, her every breath sincere, & earned.

Coda

That next off-season, Maria & Miguel
wed in the new Josh Porko Chapel.

THE PAST

It happened when the long-snapper snapped
the ball over the punter's head,
into the end zone,

& the punter, a direct descendant of General Custer's bugler,
no lie, tried getting back to at least
smother the ball

to give up just a touchback & not a touchdown, & did,
but a quarter-ton defensive tackle
cracked down on him,

elbow aimed between thin shoulderpads & helmet,
& that was that, no time even
to sound retreat

or consider other options, like chickening out, or
fumbling before the tackle
speared him....

Once dead, he did float above the scene, chin
on crossbars as stretcher-bearers
bore his body away

accompanied now not by fans' jeers or prayers but by
a bugler's notes from the prairies
of eternity.

EPILOGUE

After the injury I got a 6" pin in my foot
& steady green at the sponsor's plant in town.
I was doing real good until my blood
turned bad from mutantflu or the pin.

I fell in love with Joy, a visiting nurse.
We married the day I died.
From here I see her in her wedding veil.
I was semi-conscious for last ritual....

I banked my incentives & they grew.
I blame my death on rocketball.
Bones ain't built for what mine went through.
I wonder how Joy will spend my will.

I lived my fame to twenty-eight
which is better than most.
My end came down in prayer & vomit.
I'd rather be remembered than forgot,

but now even that thought loses feeling.
My life seems to be someone else's.
I rocket among stars with my memories,
rest my head on Joy's wedding dress.

ALLEGIANCES

The loss plunged our country into grief.
Cabbies wept at the wheel.
I pack a stun gun to protect myself.
Rebs were killed at my hotel.

I'm mum in elevators, keep my eyes down
& my mouth shut. Some psychotic
Dynamo Black clown or goon
might go ballistic.

If these are not the worst of times,
the worst of times are on their way.
The Corporation deepens plans
to reap its "Blue v. Gray."

I speak this in invisible ink
to you my invisible friend.
It's twilight here, the sun's wake
streams with scarlets & citrons.

Shall we not, while powers conspire,
swear to be true to one another?
My past is a lyric bower
glimmering absent fire.

III. THE FOOTBALL CORPORATIONS

ANTHEM FLICK

We knew about mules, as they're called,
who smuggle dope into whatever country,
like Maria in *Maria Full of Grace* who died
when bags in her stomach broke open—
we knew about mules but never expected
some bloke in the stands, when his cell vibrated,
to explode from within, I mean he wasn't strapped
or carrying a satchel he'd gotten past security but
forensics determined ferchrissakes from bits of flesh
that plastics had been inside him, detectors useless,
so now you can't tell who is going to blow himself
or herself to fucking smithereens right next to you,
John Doe or Jane Doe chock full of death.

THE CLOUD

The country wasn't going to be blackmailed,
so the 87th Super Bowl began as usual,
Sunday evening, six o'clock. Ten minutes
after speeches & anthems, his team
swelling alongside him like a wave,
Tsunami's kicker caressed the ball hard,
placed it in its tee, turned his back to it,
walked away from it, then turned to it
with a primal scream. The crowd roared,
the head ref held his arm in the air
& blew his whistle. Hundreds of millions of us
at home in our easy chairs & on our sofas
watched TV as cameras panned upward.

SPOKESPERSON

The ER was filled even before players could get there—
front-office staff, locker room attendants,
even Fritz the retired ticket-taker

who must have thought we had a game that day.
We don't know if the perpetrators
planned it this way

in order not to kill thousands, or missed their timetable.
Now for something very hard to say:
security guards

who died in the initial assault were the lucky ones—
others suffered or are suffering terribly
from the Tigris Virus—

that projectile vomiting of viscera for which there is
no known cure & which is spread by
infected dust—thus

the necessary sacrifice of our patriotic doctors & nurses
& the physical plant's vitrification
before the league resumes.

INTERIM

Inversion occurred, so that when bombs
detonated in the upper stands,

fall-out pressed down & everybody got it.
I was among those who streamed onto the field

as though artificial grass had powers to save us,
but we & the teams inhaled lethal doses....

Word is that maybe a few luckier dozens
fought their way through tunnels or locker rooms

out of that labyrinth beneath the stadium.
When the cloud lifted, our panic subsided.

Most of us got up & got home.
After x-rays, it's just a waiting game.

THE READER

I was reading. I had an intuition.
I put the book down, that nineteenth century
when the heroine with her beguiling dog
traipses across a field to visit Auntie,
picking daisies along the way.

This TV news is not romance.
Sinister plots swell from our quotidian
of hate & happenstance. But why care now?—
a death-cloud billows over prairie
toward hog-butcher Chicago. Then to me….

I've shut off the news until tonight.
Our village church bells ring to summon us
for final communion, as was our plan.
I was reading a book for the last time—
this loss, above others … breaks my heart.

AGE

I visit the nursing home—
my old lady is ninety-two.
She's one of those, you know—
her hearing's weak, her hair is blue.

We sit an hour in the solarium.
I wheel her in & set her brake—
here's fresher air than in her room,
what with Bedbound who cannot speak,

feed herself, or greet *her* son,
much less hear heaven in an aria....
I beg your pardon—her name is June,
she was a high school music teacher....

That day, Mom & I watched TV.
I cupped the news into her ear.
For half a minute, she cried wildly.
A goldfish rose for a gulp of air.

She said she'd be glad when cremated,
her ashes spread,
remembered how my father predicted
the living envying the dead—

well, it hasn't yet quite come to that
for most of us, but time
does seem to accelerate
into these football coliseums

where so much future comes to horror.
I signaled for an intern,
asked her to please make sure
my mother knew that I'd return,

then booked it, past congregations
of doctors, staff, visitors
clogging the stairs & corridors.
I drove into our age of sirens.

FOR NOW

Some heard an air-raid warning but thought nothing
of the 'copter until it kept descending
during the game.

It was maybe two-hundred feet above the players,
who were at midfield, when it
suicided down.

We speculate about whether a domed stadium
would have made a difference,
or if radar

hadn't been jammed by who knows what, but the 'copter
originated from a warehouse only
a half-mile away....

The Corporation wonders whether the score should stand until
the game can be resumed, or whether
to start over,

throw a huge memorial weekend to show those bastards
America won't be daunted.
For now,

we've just got rumors & a trivia answer: Titanium
up by six at the eight minute mark
of the third quarter.

WHERE WE WERE & WHAT WE WERE DOING

(1) Home

When our train lost power, we didn't panic.
We walked back through the tunnel,
up into light at Main and Maple.
Then, it was just a question of trying to start
our cars—electrical systems were locked—

or catching the few cabs still running.
I made it home late that evening.
My husband had the kids in bed.
I looked in on them, but did not wake them,
glad he hadn't told them anything.

(2) The Call

As we do every other Friday night,
we were playing poker in Tony's basement.

We start at eight, get pizza delivered about ten,
the cards are spread until two or three a.m.

I remember being ahead, playing good,
my hands holding up according to the odds.

When Tony's Theresa descended the stairs,
we figured she had the pizzas,

but she was white as a white bedsheet.
When Tony saw her, he stood up so fast

he knocked his chair over. His chip stacks
scattered across the table, into the muck.

Right then, my phone was ringing. It was Sam
who'd lost early and gone home.

(3) Circuitry

I worked at the Pentagon.
As far as anyone could remember,
the robotic mail-carts backtracked
for the first time ever.

(4) The News

I was raking our front lawn, bagging
red maple, ash, & sycamore leaves.
As always, I was trying to enjoy myself
within autumn's diminishing beauty,
but it was work, & I was blitzed
from drinking & poker the night before.

Neighbor Ken yelled out his front door,
"Gary, quick, catch the news."
He disappeared before I could ask him
what was up. I leaned my rake against a tree
& went inside. Step one, open yourself a beer.
Step two, another. Step three, turn on the TV.

(5) The Meat

I was on grill, right in the middle of flipping
forty-eight burgers, eight across

& six down as I like to lay them out.
I was flipping the twenty-fourth.
when I heard the explosion. My first thought,
I admit, had to do with whether or not
we'd be stuck with all this meat—
maybe I could tinfoil it, take it home,
maybe divvy it with Solly. Then the crowd
screamed past me, I near bought the farm.

(6) October

Me and Al were shooting 9-ball
at the Cabana. While he racked,
I was chalking up before my break.
He looked over past my shoulder

to the TV running the anthem sung
by all those disabled vets.
"Look," he said. I turned to see
that the whole screen was nothing but smoke,

& didn't think much of it, at first, but then
the three ex-jock announcers were screaming,
not at one another, just screaming
from the hell of it, & couldn't stop.

(7) Mountain Lake

It happened during the time it took me to drive
    to Beverage Mart a mile away
        for a couple cases of Coors,

& back—maybe twenty minutes altogether.

When I pulled into our driveway,
　　my wife ran out to meet me….

We spent the afternoon sealing off our basement
　　with insulation & duct tape.
　　　　We lived here six days, shot pool & darts until

authorities assured us the wind had veered from us.
　　Our neighbors lived the same.
　　　　We didn't have to start our generators,

didn't unseal emergency jugs of water.
　　We'll save everything for next time
　　　　which will surely come.

I'll take from this experience nothing except,
　　after the first ominous hours,
　　　　how I've accepted our situation

in this country now, and the burnt taste of the beer
　　made from Colorado water,
　　　　once pure and clear.

(8) Chaos

I was at the bank to close out one account
& start another. Two security guards
exited a back office faster than
those of us in line might have expected,

& headed for the front door. A loudspeaker
told us they'd be closing in a few minutes,
that we should please if possible postpone
transactions until the next day. Obviously,

they'd heard what had happened but
for their own reasons did not clue us in.
Most left. I decided to stay in line.
I did manage to close the one account,

& for a week when computers didn't boot,
the cash came in handy, to understate it.
So, I was lucky. Now, banking is back
to so-called normal, in god we trust.

(9) The Trucks

It was Good Neighbors Day in Smithville.
We were up at the field behind the fire hall,

behind the flea market & bake sale tables
where the volunteers had parked two trucks

& kids were scrambling up on them to learn
about extension ladders, hoses, oxygen masks,

boots, axes, all that paraphernalia employed
maybe a couple/three times a year.

We couldn't have asked for better weather,
white clouds over Lake Ontario north of us

just hovering, and our blue sky in place.
Chief Varrenti got on the loudspeaker,

told us something of what had happened.
We made our ways to our cars in good order.

Later, I'm sure, those trucks were moved,
but I keep placing them in center field.

(10) The Wish

I'd finished my thirty laps & was drying off
when word got around. I wished
I hadn't spent so much energy that day
in case our existence became
one of those apocalyptic films—

Escape from New York, Soylent Green, Rollerball—
when I'd need every ounce of strength to fill
my tank & fight my way from Brockport
to who knows where, but it didn't come
to this, not yet, not this first time.

(11) Brothers

I got into pigeons from my brother—
he raised them when we were boys.
At that time, I didn't pay attention,
just wanted to play ball every season,

but when Edwin died, I got back to our farm
where Mom & Dad still lived, & walked
those acres in apple-blossom time
to remember him. I could almost hear him

soft-talking his birds. I loaded what I could
in the way of banding equipment, cages & such,
got it to my own place here in Michigan.
I feel him with me. We won't go home again.

(12) The Reef

I rent a storage cage in the basement where I keep
    my chambered nautilus collection.

I have a radio down there, which was playing Barber's
    Adagio for Strings,

which was interrupted, no, truncated by the news.
    I got upstairs to the fourteenth floor,

then remembered I probably left the light on,
    so took the elevator back down—

no serious problems yet, but I was scared, tenants
    wedged in,

some with luggage or groceries—but we all kept calm,
    not one person screamed,

& most of us slept that night in our shells
    under the sea.

COLISEUM SOUVENIR

Both teams broke through plexiglass
dividing them before their game:
four players were killed—three stomped,

one run-through with a kneebrace shiv before
the Corporate Guard could mace & net them all.
It took a couple hours for us to settle back

into the contest designated to decide
the fate of the two ghettos where TV was blacked out
in case the old folks might go berserk.

THE STADIUM

The Corporation had it figured pretty good:
early in the week, for public relations,
inviting 50,000 firestorm victims in
who'd been stricken by hurricane-force winds
blitzing flames through their ravines.
TV featured this grateful dazed populace
downing Dynamo Reds & HugeMacs. Then,

all cameras busy elsewhere, eviction
of these homeless so that grounds crews
could prep the field for Sunday's game
which would decide which city
would be bombed. What's not to admire
about such pure cynicism? Don't
sweat it, love—I've hedged my bets.

THE FOOTBALL CORPORATIONS

First we saw just his helmet
roll out from the vicious gang-hit,
then realized that his head was still in it,

good old 44, now a gusher
who'd seldom spoken to fans before
or been injured except when his supplier

knifed him, a superficial wound, that rib-scar
he'd strum while sneering at reporters.
Anyway, when the stretcher-bearers

ran onto the field, they couldn't figure whether
to load up 44's head, or body, or both together.
I swear I don't laugh much these years,

nobody does, but for a time-out we forgot
which city would be bombed if their team lost,
which country would be forced to transport

2.5 million of its children for slave labor & food
to the other. I heard today that the blood-sod
broke Zeebay records, a square inch for a hundred grand.

Coda

44 was cremated, except for his head,
now encased in lucite at the Hall of Fame.
Visitor, straightarm your way to stand beside him.
He glares into your future like a god.

THE WARRIOR

If you want to know what it sounded like
when Stryker's neck broke,
snap a wooden creempop stick,

or, if you're living in the future when everything is plastic
& the ice cream corporation flash-freezes its plastic
vellumilla & plastic chocomarrow & plastic

bloodberry around a logo-wand of edible plastic,
just ask Cassandra, who was there with me, to crack
her knuckles, as she often does these days

even though her hands are swollen....

There. Did you hear it? The poor bastard
got hit so hard that we winced & concluded
he'd been translated into the Great Beyond,

but rumor has it he'll survive. Any chance
you'll walk Cass across the compound to her place?—
she's got welcome-girl duty for the weekend,

& I'm crucial at the heliport right now
where the CEOs are coptering in below
rogue clouds that are threatening to explode.

CAPSULE

Then came the year when seagulls flocked
into our ballparks. Stadiums without domes
postponed, then canceled even all-star games.
At first, players would play around them,
but then there were too many to kick away
or run through. We'll remember photos
of Arroyo coming up from sliding into second
with blood & feathers on his face while,
in front of the bag, the ump has one gull
by the neck, others underfoot. His call
brought both managers to the field,
& everybody laughed. Then came the year
pro football was shut down because of moths.
Then the year NASCAR tried flamethrowers
against trillions of flying ants that slicked all tracks,
but it was no use, nothing worked. Then the year
Time did not end, though we thought it would.

CENTENNIAL

It's still not clear whom
to credit for the dirty bomb
that devastated the stadium.

Should you visit, note
that no trees grow on this ground
except memorial redwoods

sheltered behind
leaded glass.
Friend, look out

through your own pane,
& don't be ashamed
to weep for gladness.

YELLOW CARD

This first World Cup on the moon:
without incendiary incident until
that signal corner kick for Axis when
their striker clappered our goalie's bell

at which time the crater exploded with grenades
maybe launched by dome security
or technicians from behind the scoreboard,
unidentified as yet (& for eternity).

So much for a distant venue where human nature
might be thwarted by distance & detectors.
Half the two teams dead or disfigured.
Pitchmen on the moon. In four years, Mars.

STORY

You knew & know the story, how What's-his-name hit
   his 3- or 5- or 7-iron
      toward a blind green, or drove it,

how he & his partner or partners looked
   everywhere for the ball, then checked the hole,
      & there it was,

it sure was, right there in the hole,
   & how his partner or partners busted his chops
      about a turtle ricochet, or about

that famous squirrel who no doubt
   retrieved the ball from a sandtrap
      & tried to plant it in the cup—

you knew & know the story except how, after
   the human depletions, something akin to this
      did happen, how legions

of squirrels dug acorns & walnuts & hickory nuts
   into greens, into even the plastic
      & steel cups that over the millennia

yielded to forest, not a trace now
   of the old courses left here in our dream
      from the end of Time.

A Note on the Author

William Heyen was born in Brooklyn, New York, in 1940. His graduate degrees are from Ohio University. A former Senior Fulbright Lecturer in American Literature in Germany, he has been honored with awards from the National Endowment for the Arts, the Guggenheim Foundation, and the American Academy of Arts and Letters. His *Crazy Horse in Stillness* won the Small Press Book Award in 1997; *Shoah Train* was a Finalist for the National Book Award in 2004; *A Poetics of Hiroshima* was a 2010 selection of the Chautauqua Literary & Scientific Circle. He is Professor of English/Poet in Residence Emeritus at his undergraduate alma mater, the College at Brockport. A list of his books appears at the front of this volume.

Books from Etruscan Press

Zarathustra Must Die | Dorian Alexander
The Disappearance of Seth | Kazim Ali
Drift Ice | Jennifer Atkinson
Crow Man | Tom Bailey
Coronology | Claire Bateman
Cinder | Bruce Bond
Peal | Bruce Bond
Toucans in the Arctic | Scott Coffel
Body of a Dancer | Renée E. D'Aoust
Nahoonkara | Peter Grandbois
The Confessions of Doc Williams & Other Poems | William Heyen
The Football Corporations | William Heyen
A Poetics of Hiroshima | William Heyen
Shoah Train | William Heyen
September 11, 2001: American Writers Respond | Edited by William Heyen
As Easy As Lying | H. L. Hix
Chromatic | H. L. Hix
First Fire, Then Birds | H. L. Hix
God Bless | H. L. Hix
Incident Light | H. L. Hix
Legible Heavens | H. L. Hix
Lines of Inquiry | H. L. Hix
Shadows of Houses | H. L. Hix
Wild and Whirling Words: A Poetic Conversation | Moderated by H. L. Hix
Art Into Life | Frederick R. Karl
Free Concert: New and Selected Poems | Milton Kessler
Parallel Lives | Michael Lind
The Burning House | Paul Lisicky
Synergos | Roberto Manzano
The Gambler's Nephew | Jack Matthews
Venison | Thorpe Moeckel
So Late, So Soon | Carol Moldaw
The Widening | Carol Moldaw
The Shyster's Daughter | Paula Priamos

Saint Joe's Passion | JD Schraffenberger
Lies Will Take You Somewhere | Sheila Schwartz
Fast Animal | Tim Seibles
American Fugue | Alexis Stamatis
The Casanova Chronicles | Myrna Stone
White Horse: A Columbian Journey | Diane Thiel
The Fugitive Self | John Wheatcroft

Etruscan Press Is Proud of Support Received From

Wilkes University

Youngstown State University

The Raymond John Wean Foundation

The Ohio Arts Council

The Stephen & Jeryl Oristaglio Foundation

The Nathalie & James Andrews Foundation

The National Endowment for the Arts

The Ruth H. Beecher Foundation

The Bates-Manzano Fund

The New Mexico Community Foundation

Founded in 2001 with a generous grant from the Oristaglio Foundation, Etruscan Press is a nonprofit cooperative of poets and writers working to produce and promote books that nurture the dialogue among genres, achieve a distinctive voice, and reshape the literary and cultural histories of which we are a part.

etruscan press
www.etruscanpress.org

Etruscan Press books may be ordered from

Consortium Book Sales and Distribution
800.283.3572
www.cbsd.com

Small Press Distribution
800.869.7553
www.spdbooks.org

Etruscan Press is a 501(c)(3) nonprofit organization.
Contributions to Etruscan Press are tax deductible
as allowed under applicable law.
For more information, a prospectus,
or to order one of our titles,
contact us at books@etruscanpress.org.